Raising confident kids

A Mindful Guide to Modeling Self-Confidence and Positive Self-Talk in kids

Peggy T. Smith

or implied. Readers acknowledge that the author is not engaging in the rendering of legal, financial, medical or professional advice. The content within this book has been derived from various sources. Please consult a licensed professional before attempting any techniques outlined in this book.

By reading this document, the reader agrees that under no circumstances is the author responsible for any losses, direct or indirect, which are incurred as a result of the use of information contained within this document, including, but not limited to, - errors, omissions, or inaccuracies.

Peggy T. Smith

Table of contents

Introduction......................................**5**

Chapter 1..............................**6**

Chapter 2..............................**14**

Chapter 3..............................**20**

Chapter 4..............................**26**

Chapter 5..............................**33**

Chapter 6..............................**39**

Conclusion........................**44**

Peggy T. Smith

Introduction

Raising confident kids is one of the most crucial duties of parenting. As parents, we want our children to grow up to be confident, capable, and well-adjusted people and nurturing self-confidence in childhood is a critical part of that process. It may be difficult to raise children who feel good about themselves and their skills, especially in a world where expectations and standards might be high. But there are numerous things that parents can do to support and foster their children's self-confidence.

One of the most essential things that parents can do to help their children develop a healthy sense of self-confidence is to be positive and supportive. Show your children that you appreciate and value them for who they are. Give them real congratulations and praise when they accomplish something and be aware of avoiding expressing too much criticism or judgment. Encourage them to take risks and attempt new things, even if it means that they could fail. Show them that you trust in their abilities to solve issues and conquer hurdles, and appreciate their efforts and triumphs.

It is also crucial to offer youngsters the chance to learn, grow, and explore. Allow them to have some autonomy and make their own decisions while being there to give direction and support.

Chapter 1

Understanding the Needs of Growing Kids

Understanding the needs of developing kids is vital to provide them with a secure, healthy, and happy environment. Kids grow and develop at various speeds, but all require love and support to realize their greatest potential. To comprehend the requirements of developing kids, parents and caregivers must be aware of the physical, cognitive, emotional, and social changes that occur at each stage of development. Parents should also be aware of any possible special needs and distinctions that may need extra assistance. Additionally, providing kids with a secure and caring environment, excellent education, and activities to cultivate skills and knowledge are crucial to helping them grow and prosper. Understanding the requirements of youngsters is consequently vital for their healthy growth and well-being. As children grow and develop, their demands will also alter and adapt. It is crucial for caregivers to be alert to these changes and to be proactive in supporting the needs of their kids. These are the key necessities for developing kids.

- **Physical needs**

Physical requirements are some of the most fundamental and vital needs that kids have. As kids grow, their physical requirements also alter. Parents must understand the physical demands of growing youngsters to maintain their best health and development. This involves giving sufficient nourishment, physical exercise, and sleep. Additionally, parents should also ensure that their children obtain adequate healthcare, including regular exams and vaccines. By knowing and supporting the physical demands of developing youngsters, parents may assist guarantee their children can attain their full potential. Growing kids have a lot of physical demands that must be satisfied for them to grow and achieve their full potential. Some of the most significant physical demands for developing kids include:

- **Nutrition**: Kids need a balanced and diverse diet to support their developing bodies and minds. This should contain lots of fruits, veggies, healthy grains, and lean meats.

- **Hydration**: Youngsters must keep hydrated, particularly during times of fast development or when they are physically active. Make sure kids have access to clean, fresh water throughout the day.

- **Sleep**: Adequate sleep is vital for kids' physical and cognitive development. Most youngsters require roughly 8-12 hours of sleep every night, depending on their age.

- **Exercise**: Regular physical exercise is vital for kids' general health and well-being. Encourage your kid to engage in a range of activities that improve physical health, such as sports, dancing, or running about outdoors.

- **Medical care**: Regular check-ups and vaccines are vital for youngsters' physical health. Make sure your kid visits a doctor or nurse frequently, and that they obtain all necessary immunizations.

- **Personal hygiene**: Teaching youngsters excellent hygiene practices, such as washing their hands frequently and cleaning their teeth, may help reduce the spread of sickness and boost overall physical health.

In conclusion, developing kids have several physical demands that must be met to maintain their optimum health and development. By satisfying these physical needs, you can help your child grow and develop in a healthy and well-rounded way.

- **Emotional needs**

Emotional requirements are another key part of kids' development. Kids require affection, attention, and a feeling of belonging to feel comfortable and connected. Growing children have specific emotional demands that need attention and care from their parents and caregivers. As children grow, their emotional development advances in comprehensive and complicated ways that are both fascinating and demanding. By understanding the emotional requirements of developing youngsters, parents may assist their children's growth and welfare.

First and foremost, kids need love, support, and security. This is particularly critical at times of transition and change, such as the beginning of school, when youngsters may feel overwhelmed and nervous. Parents should establish a secure and supportive atmosphere where their children feel welcomed and comfortable to express themselves.

As children mature, they need to have a feeling of autonomy and freedom. By enabling children to make their own decisions and choices, parents may encourage them to develop a strong sense of self-confidence and self-esteem. It is equally crucial to encourage youngsters to identify and express their emotions. Parents should help children to recognize their feelings, so that they may better understand and regulate their emotions.

Kids also need to create strong interactions with others. Parents should develop good interactions between their children and family members, friends, and peers. A child's relationship with their peers is especially important, as it helps them to develop social skills and an understanding of others.

- **Social needs**

Social needs are also important for kids' development. Kids require engagement with others, especially friendships, to feel connected and have a feeling of community. Caregivers must offer youngsters chances to engage with others and encourage them to build healthy relationships. As children grow and develop, they have a range of social requirements that must be satisfied for them to flourish. These demands may be grouped into three basic categories: social engagement, social support, and social identity.

First and foremost, developing youngsters require a social connection to learn how to communicate, empathize, and form relationships with others. This may be done through activities like playing with friends, engaging in group activities, and interacting with adults in a pleasant and supportive way. Children who do not get adequate social connections may struggle with social skills and may feel alienated or detached from others.

In addition to social engagement, developing youngsters also require social support to feel connected and valued. This might come in the form of positive reinforcement and support from adults and peers, as well as a feeling of belonging to a community or organization. Children who do not feel supported or accepted may struggle with self-esteem and confidence and may be more prone to mental health concerns such as sadness and anxiety.

Finally, developing youngsters also require a sense of social identity to feel confident and comfortable in their position in the world. This encompasses a feeling of belonging to a specific culture or group, as well as a sense of individualism and self-expression. Children who do not develop a strong sense of social identity may struggle with self-esteem and may feel detached from others.

Overall, it is crucial for developing youngsters to have their social needs satisfied to feel secure, connected, and supported. This may be attained by pleasant connections with people, a feeling of belonging, and a strong sense of identity. By satisfying these requirements, children may grow and develop into confident and well-adjusted adults.

- **Cognitive needs**

Cognitive demands are very vital for kids' growth. Kids are continuously learning and exploring their environment, and caregivers must offer them chances to do so. This might involve giving children age-appropriate toys, books, and other learning tools, and encouraging them to ask questions and investigate their world. Growing youngsters require a range of cognitive experiences to help them attain their greatest potential. Cognitive activities such as problem-solving, reasoning, and critical thinking help youngsters learn how to think, analyze, and make choices. These activities also help students establish crucial life skills and learn information that may be utilized in the future.   Additionally, offering chances to exercise memory and attention skills may assist youngsters to develop concentration, focus, and concentration. Finally, enabling children to explore and experiment in a secure and supportive atmosphere may help them develop higher-level thinking abilities.

Understanding the needs of developing youngsters is a continuous process that involves patience, understanding, and support. It is crucial to establish an atmosphere where children feel secure, loved, and respected. Through open communication, establishing clear expectations, and offering advice and support, parents may help youngsters grow into healthy, responsible, and successful adults.

Chapter 2

Positive Reinforcement

Positive reinforcement is a useful strategy to utilize while developing confident youngsters. It is a method of behavior modification that rewards excellent conduct with positive attention, praise or physical prizes such as stickers or points. This strategy helps youngsters learn to correlate good actions with incentives, which encourages them to continue participating in those activities. Positive reinforcement also enables youngsters to experience achievement, which enhances their self-esteem and helps them build the confidence to attempt new activities... Here are some strategies to utilize positive reinforcement to enhance your child's confidence:

- **Give particular praise**

Specific praise is a vital component of growing confident youngsters. Rather than merely saying "nice work," be precise about what you are appreciating. For example, "I truly admired how you asked for assistance when you were struggling with that arithmetic issue. That displays independence and problem-solving skills." Some such instances of particular commendation include:

1. "You did a terrific job finding out how to answer that arithmetic problem!"
2. "I'm proud of you for speaking out in class today."
3. "I appreciate how you persisted with it and practiced until you got it right."
4. "Your hard work paid off - you should be pleased with yourself!"
5. "You have such a lovely heart - I'm so delighted you shared your food with your friend."
6. "You worked so hard on that project - you should be proud of what you've accomplished."

- **Use rewards**

Rewards might be simple things like stickers or tiny toys, or they can be more big, like extended screen time or a special excursion. Just be careful to reward behaviors that you want to see more of, rather than penalizing undesirable actions. Using incentives in raising confident kids may be an effective technique for teaching desirable behaviors and reinforcing good habits. Rewards may be used to inspire children to do the right thing, to help them understand the value of having goals and working towards them, and to celebrate their successes. Rewards may also assist youngsters to learn to accept responsibility for their behavior and create self-esteem.

Rewards may come in numerous ways, such as verbal appreciation, material things, or a particular privilege. The trick is to pick incentives that are relevant and suitable for the child's age and development. For example, a young kid may require a sticker or a tiny toy after accomplishing a chore properly, while an older child may need a greater reward, such as a trip to the movies or a special adventure. When utilizing prizes to promote desirable actions, it's crucial to remember that they should be utilized sparingly and regularly. If incentives are utilized too regularly, children may begin to anticipate them, and the intended behavior may not be maintained. Also, it's vital to bear in mind that awards should be based on the child's effort, not their performance. The rewarding effort helps youngsters learn that hard work pays off and may help them become more confident and resilient.

- **Use positive language**

Avoid criticizing and instead concentrate on the good parts of your child's behavior. For example, instead of stating "You're so clumsy," say "I saw that you did your best to balance on that beam. Good effort!".

A positive language is a key tool for nurturing confident youngsters. It entails communicating with children in a courteous, encouraging, and validating manner. Parents should also use encouraging words and phrases, such as "I believe in you," "You can do it," and "You are capable." This style of language promotes an atmosphere of acceptance and trust, which helps youngsters develop a feeling of security and a good self-image. Additionally, it increases resilience and teaches youngsters how to self-regulate their emotions. Positive language also helps youngsters grow to be sympathetic, as they learn to perceive and express the feelings of others. Finally, it helps youngsters learn to accept responsibility for their actions and choices.

- **Encourage effort**

Rather than merely praising your kid for being clever or gifted, reward them for their hard work and effort. This will let children recognize that their talents are something they can grow through practice. An encouraging effort is a terrific technique to help youngsters acquire confidence. Praise their hard work and effort, rather than their skill, and encourage them to take chances and try new things. Encouraging youngsters to take on difficulties and offering support and direction encourages them to build a feeling of achievement and self-confidence. Set reasonable expectations and give good reinforcement. Help them realize that errors are part of learning and tell them to continue to work hard and remain motivated.

- **Offer options**

Giving your youngster options makes them feel more in control and might increase their confidence. For example, rather than prescribing what they should wear, ask "Which shirt do you want to wear today, the blue one or the green one?"

Offering alternatives is a terrific method to help youngsters develop more confidence. Giving children the chance to make their own choices may help them develop a feeling of self-efficacy, as they grow in their knowledge of how their actions can lead to good consequences. Choices may be minor, such as enabling them to choose the dress they want to wear or the food they want for breakfast. As children develop, so can their options, enabling them to make greater selections, such as which after-school activity to join in, or where to go for vacation. This may help children learn to trust their judgment and create self-confidence.

Overall, positive reinforcement helps youngsters feel valued and encourages them to take chances and try new activities. This may lead to improved confidence and a readiness to take on new tasks.

Chapter 3

Teaching Kids to Believe in Themselves

Teaching youngsters to believe in themselves is a crucial element of parenting and schooling. Children who have a high sense of self-confidence and self-esteem are more likely to be successful in school, relationships, and other aspects of life.

As parents, when you have more than one kid, particularly with an age range of 3-5 years you can detect the difference in their actions. Everything one does is distinct from the other. This age difference is significant in understanding how youngsters when growing up prefer to learn and reflect by seeing adults. In a child's first three years, he/she establishes views and expectations of themselves, choosing whether he/she is significant, if he/she is loved, and if he/she is competent. By the time toddlers are three years old, youngsters have a solid way of perceiving themselves with labels like "short or tall," "boy or girl," or "good or bad." Now that it's evident that your response may primarily affect your children, ask yourself this: "Are you a parent that reacts to day-to-day problems which your kid goes through optimistically?"

Imagine your youngster on a sports day, he/she is all ready for their big day. You gave them new sneakers and they are thrilled to run. You are at the school playground, sitting in the stands watching them take a position and even you are delighted and want to scream for them in a loud voice. You greatly desire that they finish first. The moment has arrived. All contestants have taken their place. The referee is poised to sound the whistle. As the time arrives, you as a parent are beginning to develop conflicting thoughts about the race now. Suddenly all you hear is the unsettling sound of the whistle and in absolutely no time you can see your youngster rushing on the muddy tracks. You are enthusiastic yet anxious at the same time. While you roll your eyes in the direction of the finish line in rhythm with your child you see him fall, he gets up and is now much behind everyone else. He seeks you amid a vast number of people cheering in the stands. You glance at him and notice that he is staring at you with a low spirit. The race is ended, and he finishes but last. You are driving home and while chatting about what had transpired, your youngster is upset and quite dejected about what happened and blames himself. How will you handle this situation?

Having good self-esteem is vital as your kid grows up. As your kid grows older, he/she will encounter numerous problems, and having high self-esteem is vital for making safe and healthy decisions. Thus, it is vitally crucial for your youngster to feel he/she is worth a lot. It is inarguable that a kid is more likely to develop high self-esteem when his/her parents are kind and nurturing, expressing via their actions and words that they are valuable and competent.

While parents must play an active part in increasing their child's self-confidence, parents also need to educate their children on how to take responsibility for their sentiments and sense of self-esteem and most important teach hygiene from an early age. Providing your kid with this knowledge and assistance can help give him the confidence and decision-making abilities required to have a good sense of self-esteem which minimizes chances for social, emotional, and academic challenges. How can parents, families, and caregivers guarantee that they foster the development of children's self-esteem?

- **Demonstrate and demonstrate a real interest in your children:**

By displaying a real interest in your children you not only get to be friends with them but you also indirectly show them that you care about their likes, dislikes, and other perspectives about life.

- **Engage children in age-appropriate activities that enhance problem-solving:**

A mistake that most parents try to make is pushing their children into their likes and dislikes. You should rather choose for allowing your youngster to pursue his hobbies and be free from unwarranted external pressure. This does not imply that you cease caring. You always provide a hand when he needs one the most.

- **Tell your kid when you feel proud of him/her:**

Parents are frequently ready to convey unpleasant thoughts to their kids, but for some reason disclose their happy feelings with greater difficulty. Your kid isn't always clear when you are feeling pleased with him/her, therefore they particularly need to hear from you regularly that you're delighted with them and their actions & decisions. Children remember the nice things we tell them. They store them up and repeat our positive words to themselves, which helps them feel cherished and desired.

- **Use a positive method for creating limits and consequences for your child:**

All children need to take responsibility for their actions, and developing self-discipline is a very crucial component of growing up. To assist children to acquire self-discipline, the parent should approach their involvement in this part of their child's development by behaving as a coach/teacher, rather than a disciplinarian/punisher. While you are fair, tough, and kind when dealing with your kid, you will help them take responsibility for their conduct (both bad and good) without making them feel awful and guilty about their behavior. They need to learn from their errors and not be criticized for them.

- **Laugh with your children and encourage them to laugh at themselves.**

This is extremely crucial to guarantee your youngster grows his/her self-confidence. People who take themselves too seriously are undoubtedly losing out on a lot of fun in life! A good sense of humor and the capacity to laugh at oneself is crucial. Make sure you lead by example and let your kids know it's all right to laugh at your blunders! Apart from these things, there are a few common things that you do that might assist your youngster to believe in themselves:

Give genuine, positive comments rather than hollow praise and flattery, elaborating on the achievement that you are talking about rather than simply stating "good job", being a positive role model, displaying positivity, honesty, and compassion so your children may replicate your good conduct, helping your kid establish good views about himself, whether they be about his looks, his abilities, or his accomplishments, creating a secure, caring home and family atmosphere.

Additionally, the objective of this is to educate parents so that they maintain supporting their children and let them know that they need to trust themselves. This stimulates them and offers them a greater capacity to think constructively by making use of positive thinking abilities when presented with difficulty. In addition, encouraging them makes them more resilient and this helps them to effectively execute and accomplish their jobs.

Chapter 4

Encouraging Kids to Take Risks

It's extremely normal for parents to want to protect their children from harm at all costs, but it's also healthy and natural for youngsters to want to take chances and explore the world around them. Children typically learn by trying new things, and risk-taking is part of that.

Taking chances may boost a child's confidence as they overcome anxieties and find they are capable in ways they may not have known previously. There are, of course, limitations to the sorts of risks children at this age may take, and it mostly relies on how comfortable you as a parent feel with the balance of risk and rewards connected with the activities, but it's vital to try to keep in mind that risks can be good for children too. Keep in mind that many things that may appear little to you might be scary for your youngster since they're unclear how things will end out. Some youngsters are more risk-averse than others, while some may seem to take chances to an extreme. Those youngsters may be more impulsive or immature and may need to be cautioned about consequences more than other children. The Director of the Rutgers Social-Emotional Learning Lab Maurice Elias says that you strive to stress your displeasure over an abstract consequence since it is more likely to make sense to your kid. For example, stating, "You have to hold my hand or walk close next to me when we're in a crowd. If we got separated you may get lost and I would be extremely terrified and worried," instead saying, "A stranger might kidnap you," focuses the concern on you and not on your child.

When youngsters can venture out of their comfort zone, it's a risk. Allowing your kid to take risks offers her a little excitement of the unknown — they haven't brought the dog into the backyard alone before. Will the dog respond to them when they call? For younger children, taking a risk might be as easy as being active in class by raising a hand to answer a question. It may be as basic as a first overnight or a new playdate. Making a new acquaintance may also be a type of risk-taking for youngsters this age. Perhaps a new student enters their class, or maybe they are the new student. Taking that initial step, introducing yourself, and attempting to make a friend may be nerve-racking and a little intimidating, but when the other kid smiles back and they begin a discussion, they may feel pleased with themself for taking the initiative. Age-appropriate risk-taking may be highly useful for your child's feeling of self-confidence and can teach them that even when the result is unpredictable, sometimes a risk is worth taking. Try to bear in mind that every risk has the potential for both success and disaster. Learning typically comes through trial and error and learning from errors. Allowing your kid to fail (without long-term damage or injury) is vital for developing tenacity and grit.

When a youngster comes face-to-face with a new scenario, whether it's a foreign meal, a physical challenge, or strange people, he may experience true sensations of dread, anxiety, helplessness, and vulnerability. New settings are unexpected to youngsters and threaten their desire to feel comfortable and in control. Their desire to give something new a try and take a positive, safe risk despite an uncertain result is greatly impacted by your response at the moment.

As parents, what should you do when your kid is afraid to take a risk? How can you assist and gently urge him to try something new before he chooses to fully give up? Here are some do's and don'ts to adhere to while assisting your youngster to take the jump:

- **Mirror and Validate Feelings**:
If your kid is frightened to take a risk, listen to what he is expressing and acknowledge his anxieties while giving empathy and support. Try expressing "I can tell in your face that you are scared. It's acceptable to feel that way! But I am here to assist keep you safe!" or "You don't want to attempt that right now. That's alright. Let's step back and observe for a few minutes." Staying clued into your child's emotions and normalizing his sentiments teaches him that you hear and understand him. If he believes you are there to guide him through his emotions and he feels supported, he will become courageous enough to give it a try.

- **Don't Force It, Yet Don't Immediately Give Up.**
Forcing your child to do anything by kicking and screaming is never recommended. Children won't suddenly grow to enjoy something, nor will they be encouraged to try again if they have been coerced into doing something they don't want to do. If you push your kid to do anything before he is ready, you risk forming a bad connection with that activity or even inducing trauma, which may lead to deeply

rooted-anxieties that may be hard to overcome in the future. Who needs more treatment to save for?

You may find a balance between being too firm and too slack with kind and encouraging remarks such as, "This seems hard, but we are going to attempt to complete it. Let's take a break and come back to try again" or "It might seem terrifying to taste a new meal. You need to taste, but you can spit it out if you don't like it." It's crucial to be patient, but persistent.

- **Do Help Your Child Feel In Control:**
Since new experiences are unexpected and dangerous, let your youngster feel more in control of the situation by providing him with plenty of options. "We can stand to the side for 2 or 3 more rotations, and then it will be your chance to attempt! What do you choose? 2 or 3?" or "How many minutes would you prefer to wait before you give it a try? 4 or 5 minutes?" Even asking your kid where he would want you to stand, watch or wait, or whether or not he needs your support can empower him and make him feel more secure in the circumstance.

- **Don't Try To Reason:**

When a youngster is filled with enormous sensations, attempting to talk him into doing anything is often fruitless. Telling a youngster he would enjoy it, or that it's so fun, or that all his friends are doing it isn't getting to the core of the problem which is that he is anxious and terrified. In such instances, your reasoning will only serve to annoy, rather than encourage your youngster. Instead of attempting to "prove" to your youngster how fantastic something is, remember to identify and stay with the sentiments at the moment. Providing reassurance that he will be secure, that you are there to support him, and that it's alright to experience his emotions is what will encourage him to overcome his fear and take a risk.

- **Do Circle Back After A Success.**

Once your youngster gets up the bravery to attempt something new, it is cause for celebration! Take a few minutes to restate to your kid what has happened: "You were so frightened to go down that large waterside, but you accomplished it! And you are safe and it was fun!" Connecting the dots and re-telling the narrative helps your kid to gather and construct his database of experiences to rely upon when he is presented with yet another danger. He will recall, "I felt this way previously when I did that large waterslide and I was alright! I bet it will be the same this time too." Confidence grows with experience and you can help your child collect positive experiences by supporting him through each risk.

Remember, you are your child's best example, so if you'd like him to grow more comfortable trying new things be sure that you are also modeling positive risk-taking and providing ample opportunities to stretch limits in addition to being present and emotionally in tune with your child. Ultimately the hope in encouraging your child to try new things is that he will learn much about his limits, grow in confidence and experience, and become more open and willing to take future positive risks.

Chapter 5

Helping Kids Overcome Challenges

Helping kids to overcome problems is a crucial job for parents, carers, and educators. Children confront several problems as they grow and develop, from acquiring new skills to navigating social interactions and relationships. Many parents are on a mission to help their children succeed and desire to shield them from any problems or setbacks in their life. It's frequently tough for parents to see their children confront difficulties that may be unpleasant and distressing. Although it may be easier said than done, parents should bear in mind that they cannot shelter their children from every difficulty and that confronting problems is a crucial part of a child's growth and ability to attain success. Rather than shielding their children from hurdles, parents can consider utilizing these challenges as tools to help their children grow resilience and create good coping methods for those times when they feel discouraged or irritated. How can parents assist their children to overcome hurdles and accomplish their goals? Here are a few suggestions:

- **Encourage them to take little moves**

Rather than overwhelming them with enormous activities, break difficulties down into smaller, achievable stages. This can help students feel more secure and successful as they strive towards their objectives.

- **Understand Feelings & Emotions**

As children grow and mature, they encounter new sensations like rage, defeat, and frustration. Parents must lead their children through their emotions and assist them to learn how to express their feelings healthily. Rather than saving them from experiencing anger, frustration, or defeat, give them space to go through these feelings and know when to step in with recommendations and next actions. Parents may help their children as they learn how to process their emotions and acknowledge their experiences. When children have a better awareness of their emotions they will more likely be able to manage their feelings, create resilience, and develop a strong sense of determination. Emotional intelligence may help youngsters handle problems with confidence as they strive toward realizing their aspirations

• Lead by Example

It's no secret that children learn from their environment. That's why parents must provide a positive example for their children, even when they feel angry, irritated, or dejected. Children typically study how their parents respond to hard events and use it as guidance in their own life. If a youngster witnesses their parent's fear during a hard scenario, or yell when they're furious, they will most likely repeat such actions. If a youngster sees that their parent is easily defeated or scared by problems, they are prone to share those same attitudes. When confronting obstacles, parents should attempt to provide a positive example for their children by exhibiting resolve and behaving maturely and appropriately. Many parents shy away from discussing their struggles with their children while in truth, sharing challenges, and reactions to failures, and the results are a great approach to educating youngsters on how to be resilient. As many people would agree, confronting problems and overcoming hurdles are vital parts of attaining our objectives. Parents must assist their children to attain their objectives by providing a good example when it comes to handling emotions and problems. Help them develop problem-solving skills: Teaching youngsters how to spot issues and come up with solutions can help them feel more competent and confident when presented with obstacles.

- **Encourage them to seek assistance**

If a youngster is suffering from an issue, it is crucial to encourage them to seek assistance. This might be from a parent, teacher, or another trustworthy adult. It's normal for youngsters to confront problems as they grow and develop. As a parent or caregiver, it's crucial to be helpful and encouraging when your kid is confronting a hardship. Helping your kids seek aid might come in various forms including encouraging your child to speak about their thoughts and problems. By listening to your kid and expressing that you care about their challenges, you may help them feel heard and supported. Helping people recognize and exploit their abilities. Encourage your kid to concentrate on their strengths and good attributes, and help them discover ways to utilize these abilities to overcome obstacles.

1. Encouraging your youngster to take pauses and exercise self-care. Youngsters must take pauses and participate in activities that help them relax and rejuvenate. This may include things like getting lots of sleep, exercising,

and participating in hobbies and activities they like.

2. Providing resources and help. Depending on the problem your kid is experiencing, it could be good to give them extra resources or assistance. This might involve finding a tutor or mentor, enrolling in a class or workshop, or seeking the advice of a therapist or counselor.

3. Being patient and understanding. Remember that your kid is still learning and developing, and it's normal for them to confront problems. Be patient and understanding while they work through these issues, and try to avoid being critical or judgemental.

4. Encouraging them to create objectives and strive towards them. Help your kid establish realistic objectives and help them to build a strategy for reaching those goals. This might help them feel more secure and motivated as they attempt to solve their obstacles.

- **Help Them See the "Bigger Picture"**

Parents may assist their children to overcome problems by urging them to view the "bigger picture." Children frequently live in the now and when a time in their life becomes tough, they can't always see the light at the end of the tunnel. Maybe one of their school tasks is very tough, or maybe they are having problems learning how to perform a new song on their instrument, these minor barriers may make youngsters feel defeated and disappointed. During these trying times, parents must remind their children about the significance of hard effort and the reward, or sense of achievement, that comes with it. For some youngsters, it might be useful to divide the task down into smaller stages to accomplish the eventual objective. Parents should remind their children of their ultimate aims to help keep them motivated so that they may work through their problems and accomplish their ambitions!

In conclusion, helping kids overcome problems may be a challenging but rewarding undertaking for parents and caregivers. It is crucial to stay patient, empathetic, and supportive while also encouraging youngsters to discover their answers and build their resilience. By teaching kids coping skills, creating clear limits, and providing a secure and supportive environment, we can help them tackle obstacles straight on and emerge stronger and more confident people.

Chapter 6

Teaching Problem-Solving Skills

Why Problem-Solving Skills Matter?

Kids experience a range of obstacles every day, ranging from scholastic difficulties to troubles on the sports field. Yet few of them have a formula for fixing such challenges. Kids who lack problem-solving abilities may delay taking action when presented with a challenge. Rather than investing their efforts into fixing the problem, they may concentrate their time on avoiding the issue. That's why many youngsters lag in school or struggle to maintain friendships.

Other youngsters who lack problem-solving abilities jump into action without understanding their options. A youngster may punch a classmate who cuts in front of them in line since they do not know what else to do. Or, they may walk out of class while they are being taunted since they can't think of any other methods to make it stop. Those rash actions may produce even larger issues in the long term.

Kids who feel overwhelmed or despondent generally won't try to solve a situation. But when you provide kids with a clear strategy for addressing difficulties, they'll feel more confident in their capacity to attempt. Here are the stages of problem-solving:

- **Identify the issue:**
Just addressing the situation out loud may make a tremendous impact on youngsters who are feeling trapped. Help your kid articulate the issue, such as, "You don't have someone to play with at recess," or "You aren't sure whether you should take the advanced math class."

- **Develop at least five potential answers:**
Brainstorm various methods to fix the situation. Emphasize that all the answers don't necessarily need to be excellent ideas (at least not at this time) (at least not at this point). Help your youngster discover solutions if they are struggling to come up with ideas. Even a foolish response or far-fetched concept is a feasible solution. The trick is to make

them recognize that with a little ingenuity, they may uncover many other viable answers.

- **Identify the benefits and drawbacks of each option:**
Help your kid identify possible good and negative effects for each potential solution they considered.

- **Pick a solution:**
Once your kid has analyzed the various good and bad effects, encourage them to select a solution.
Test it out. Tell them to attempt a solution and see what occurs. If it doesn't work out, they may always attempt another idea from the list that they generated in step two.

- **Use problem solving techniques:**
When challenges develop, don't hurry to fix your child's problems for them. Instead, assist them to move through the problem-solving stages. Offer direction when they need aid, but encourage them to handle challenges on their own. If they are unable to come up with a solution, jump in and assist them to think of some. But don't immediately tell them what to do. When you confront behavioral challenges, utilize a problem-solving strategy. Sit down together and explain, "You've been having problems getting your schoolwork done recently.

Let's problem-solve this collectively." You may still need to deliver a penalty for misbehaving, but make it apparent that you're involved in searching for a solution so they can do better next time.

"Use a problem-solving technique to assist your youngster to grow more autonomous".

If kids forget to carry their soccer cleats for practice, ask, "What can we do to make sure this doesn't happen again?" Let them attempt to create some solutions on their own. Kids frequently create inventive solutions. So they could say, "I'll write a note and place it on my door so I'll remember to pack them before I go," or "I'll pack my bag the night before and I'll make a checklist to remind me what has to go in my bag." Provide lots of praise as your youngster practices their problem-solving abilities.

- **Allow for Natural Consequences**

Natural consequences may also teach problem-solving abilities. So when it's appropriate, let your kid confront the natural repercussions of their conduct. Just be sure it's safe to do so. For example, let your adolescent spend all of their money within the first 10 minutes you're at an amusement park if that's what they want. Then, let them go for the remainder of the day without any spending money.

This might lead to a talk about problem-solving to help them make a better decision next time. Consider these natural outcomes as a learning opportunity to help work together on problem-solving.

Conclusion

Raising confident kids is a crucial job for every parent. It is crucial to offer your children a secure and supportive atmosphere that encourages them to communicate their ideas, emotions, and wishes. Encourage your children to take chances and attempt new things, even if they don't always succeed. Teach your children to be resilient and embrace errors as part of learning. Help children to build strong social skills by demonstrating excellent conduct and mentoring them in areas such as communication and teamwork. Model strong self-esteem and positive body language to teach your children that they can do everything they put their minds to. Provide children with the opportunity to explore their interests and abilities and to create their sense of identity. Allow children to make their judgments and choices and to take control of their learning. Show them that failure is part of the learning process and that it may be a fantastic chance to progress.

Finally, remind your children that you love and support them completely and that you are always there for them. With these techniques and your love and direction, you can help your children become confident and successful persons.